Doodling for Cat Lovers

Copyright © 2020 Tony R. Smith All Rights Reserved.

No part of this publication may be reproduced, distributed, or transmitted in any form or by any means, including photocopying, recording, or other electronic or mechanical methods, or by any information storage and retrieval system without the prior written permission of Smith Show Publishing, except in the case of very brief quotations embodied in critical reviews and certain other noncommercial uses permitted by copyright law.

Tell us about your Cat

_____

_____

_____

_____

_____

_____

_____

_____

HOW TO DOODLE USING THE CIRCLE METHOD.

Draw two circles. The circles will be your head and body of your cat.

Draw a fun face and ears. Next, draw some simple feet for your cool cat.

Draw some simple deigns on the body of your cat.

Erase the circle patterns. Your cat drawing is complete.

HOW TO DOODLE IN THREE EASY STEPS.

Step 1

Draw a fun simple head. Make it simple.

Step 2

Now, lets work on the cat body. Make simple curves and circles.

Step 3

Lets finish your doodle. Draw simple feet to help complete your drawing.

Cat faces......

Draw on the next page

More cat faces...

Draw on the next page

Last of the cat faces...

Draw on the next page

Do you.....

Draw me on the next page

Can your cat.....

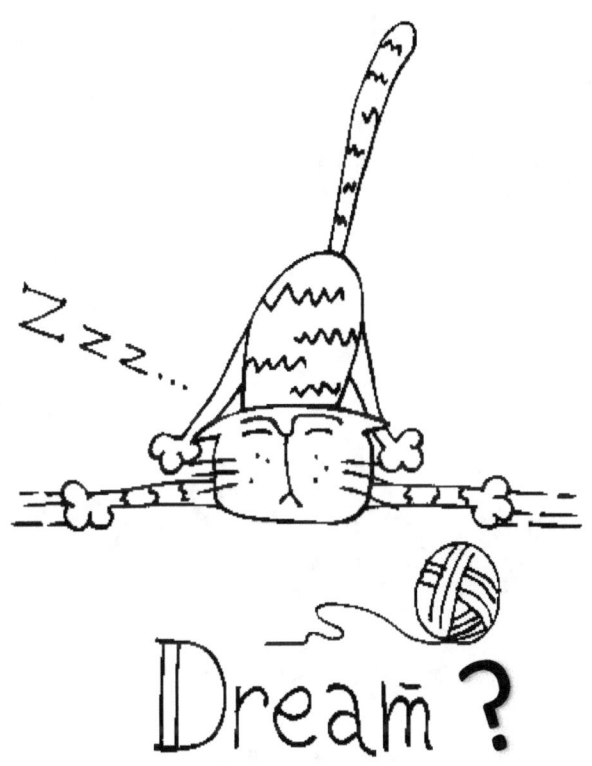

Draw me on the next page

This is my.....

Draw me on the next page

I need food now!

Draw me on the next page

Watch out below.

Draw me on the next page

Feed me or leave me alone!

Draw me on the next page

Can I have some help?

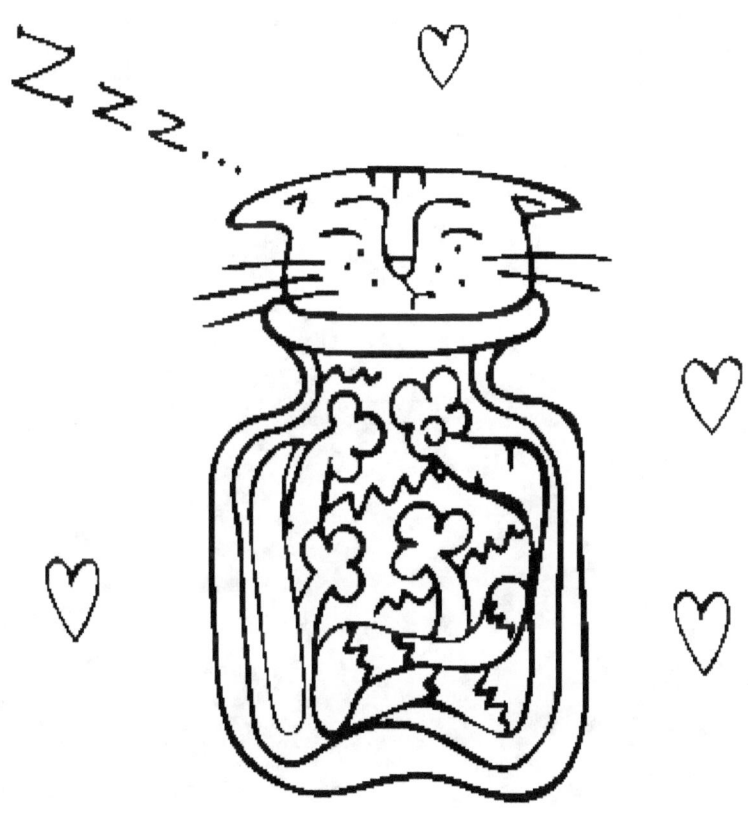

Draw me on the next page

HAVE A GOOD TIME

Draw me on the next page

I can walk on the wild side.

Draw us on the next page

I need attention please.

Draw us on the next page

Read my body language.

Draw us on the next page

Draw us on the next page

We love to drink.

Draw us on the next page

We stick together.

Draw us on the next page

Three is better than one.

Draw us on the next page

One big happy family.

Draw us on the next page

I love my baby kitty.

Draw us on the next page

I love twins cats.

Draw us on the next page

He is so cute.

Draw us on the next page

Draw me on the next page

Reading is fundamental.

Draw us on the next page

Draw us on the next page

It's kitty love all-day.

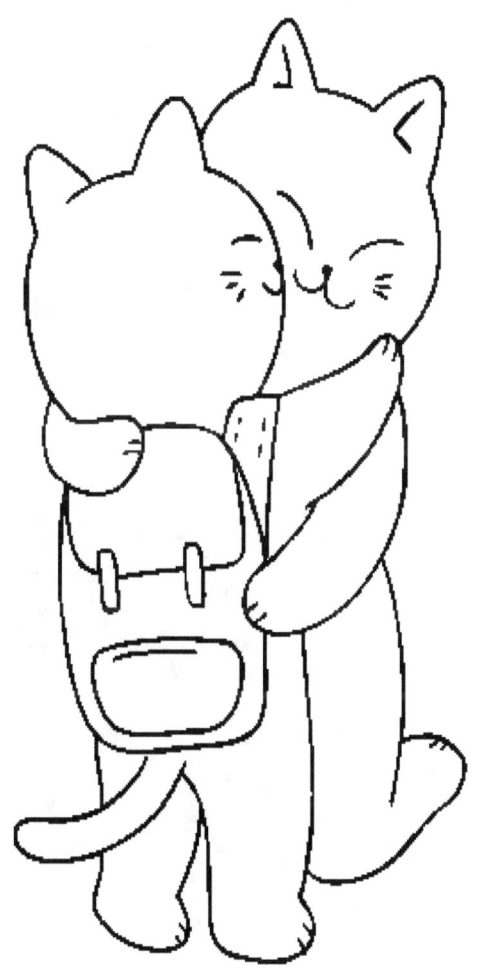

Draw us on the next page

Good night my cat

Draw us on the next page

Night time is fun.

Draw us on the next page

Draw m2 on the next page

Cute as can be.

Draw us on the next page

Draw me on the next page

Time for a nap.

Draw me on the next page

Life in the sun is cool.

Draw us on the next page

Triple the fun.

Draw us on the next page

Yes....we have friends.

Draw us on the next page

Life is a beach.

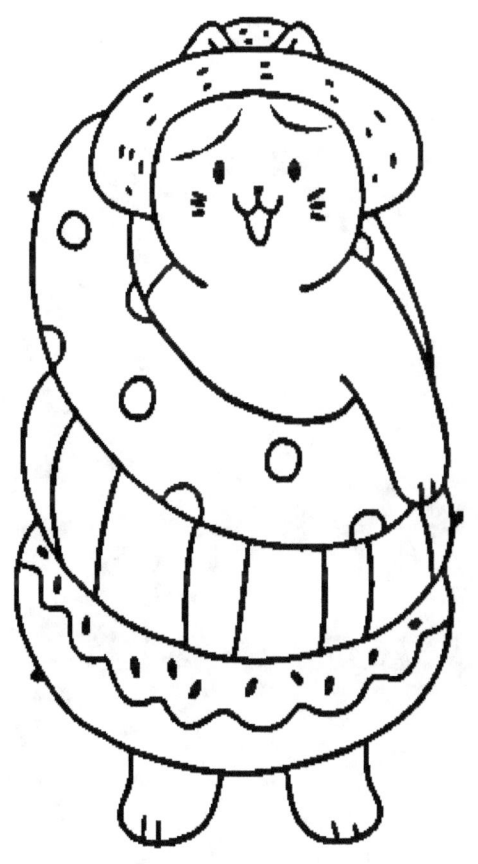

Draw me on the next page

Fun in the sun.

Draw us on the next page

Yes...I'm cute.

Draw me on the next page

Lunch anyone?

Draw me on the next page

Grilled food is the best!

Draw us on the next page

Family vacation.

Draw us on the next page

Cats and ice cream.

Draw us on the next page

Cats in the sand.

Draw us on the next page

Sleepy Sunday at the beach.

Draw me on the next page

I love pillows.

Draw me on the next page

Draw me on the next page

Time to eat.

Draw me on the next page

Draw us on the next page

We love trips.

Draw us on the next page

Draw us on the next page

DRAW YOUR VISION

DRAW YOUR VISION

DRAW YOUR VISION

DRAW YOUR VISION

DRAW YOUR VISION

www.ingramcontent.com/pod-product-compliance
Lightning Source LLC
Chambersburg PA
CBHW052111110526
44592CB00013B/1568